The Magic Outside

Written by De-Ann Kelly

Illustrated by Beth Mcnamarra

ISBN: 978-976-96640-0-5

It's beautiful outside, so outside we go.
All the magical creatures are putting on a show.
The plants are swaying from side to side.
Today let's just seek instead of hide.

Let's seek out the treasures in our big garden - flowers, leaves, bugs;
they are all such charmers.

I can hear the birds chirping, it seems they are calling us.
Let's hurry outside so they won't make a fuss.

I can see the birds now that we are outside,
I love to watch them fly they do it with such pride.
They are yellow and blue with red on their heads,
they spread their wings wide from each flower bed.

I hear bees buzzing, bzzz, it sounds so funny.
Wouldn't it be nice if they make us some honey?

I feel something crawling on my hand and it tickles.
Oh look! It's a ladybug, I can't help but giggle.

Ladybugs protect our garden from little biting insects,
the ones that feast on our plants til there're no leaves left.

The dandelions aim to reach as high as the sky
and we can see the butterflies fly gracefully by.

Look at all the flowers, I can get a great view.
There are daisies, roses, chrysanthemums too.
They sparkle in pink, white, orange, and purple.
Their loose petals blow up, down and around in a circle.

The wind whispers in my ear, I can hear it clear.
It says "Hey, nice to see you today. Isn't the day fair?".

We water the plants and take out the weeds,
tomorrow we'll be back to plant some new seeds.

I'm glad you came and played with us today.
The magic outside was really worth the stay.

About the Author

De-Ann Kelly is an island girl with an unrelenting love for nature. Born and raised in Jamaica, she enjoys spending her time outdoors admiring the sea, sky and sand adorned by the sun, beautiful plants, exotic birds, brilliant butterflies and the majestic rivers the island boasts. It's only right that The Magic Outside is her first published book.